CAPTURE & FLIGHT

Capture & Flight

LINNET HUNTER

Wild Sky

Published by Wild Sky Publishing
A division of BCBG PTY LTD
Birregurra, Victoria, Australia

Copyright © 2021 by Linnet Hunter

All rights reserved. No part of this book may be reproduced in any manner whatsoever without written permission except in the case of brief quotations embodied in critical articles and reviews.

First edition, 2016 Second edition, 2021
Cover art and design by Rebecca Readhead

dedicated to my children
M
F
&
J
who are the sunshine of my life
and the starlight I write by

WHITE BIRDS

white birds
wheel in flight
above a lighted tower

drawn, repulsed
unable to alight

they turn and turn
weaving winged patterns of unending knots

I am and am not
a bird – my wings
were made to soar in further
reaches

I too am drawn
to worship at that
tower of light

held in the hypnotic glare
of its full phallic strength

the tower light casts only shadow on my soul
and gives no rest

promising pleasure and giving

unceasing desire

BOUND

love seemed a toy
a harmless ball of shining twine

and like a kitten, I patted
and rolled it

never seeing how its silken webs
floated wide
and gently,
invisibly,
tied themselves
about my limbs

till I was caught
in fine fine lines
of gleaming mesh

bound
into docility

I gaze in wonder
as these heartstrings

play out in gleaming wires of light
about and around me

I fool no more with what I cannot know

FISHING

leaf and blossom
bloom and bud
does it drive you crazy?
he asked

that quizzical baiting
need to know
alive and still burgeoning
in the growing spring of his fiftieth year

no
she could have replied

but didn't

resisted for the first time the sparkling lures
dancing in the sunshine of his listening face

refused to bite
disdained the bait
ignored the line

swam past it with a flashing fin

he drew it in empty...
but kept it to cast on another day

FLY WILD

you

have awakened my heart
and set it free

to fly wild
like a bird

why then,

do I
return to your door
seeking crumbs?

IT DID NOT

your fingertips touched me
-softer than rain petals

your lips brushed my skin
 - gentler than rose drops

inside your embrace
-stronger than castle walls

I was melded to your skin
 - sanctuary

it did not
frighten me
as it was wont to do

no, it did not

why did no warning bells ring out?

no siren pain awaken me to dread

that I might lose so soon what I had wished for?

but, it did not.

I half slumbered on
trusting that the next kiss would come

yet,

                    it did not

SHALL I WAIT ON?

I am the princess woken by
a word

I am the frog unkissed

I am Rapunzel, shorn and lonely
in the tower

I am a witch who waits
to taste innocence

shall I be freed?

or could I, myself,
who am both guard and
guardian of the gate

unlock that bar?

LONELINESS

in loneliness
the silence of noise
grows

a buzz saw whining
with the fear
of
loneliness itself

behind the
bars of anxiety
in solitary confinement
I await release

into another silence

LIKE A THIEF

like a thief
I creep,
sullenly,
onto the land
home of my soul
barred to me
to me by your resentment

the gate swings heavily -
the chicken house lies empty
neglected while you mourned me

the scented herbs are rank with weeds
the dogs, deserted, howl and yap for my attention
but I am desperate in haste to take what is mine,
steal glances, perfumes, sights

and be gone
before any can call me to account

vases broken, plates chipped, lamps cracked
all the remnants of a home seem to clutter
my thoughts with domestic disaster
 - a crack in the ceiling plaster where you heaved a fist,
 - a broken curved moon of missing paint where that
glass hit the wall

these are the things I left

but never will I leave
that chocolate earth
those undulations of full-flowered grasses in the wind
or the dappled leaf of tulip tree and maple
birch and walnut

they are part of me now
and from myself, there can be
no unleaving

your world retreats into itself
as mine expands

bitterness drains away into the loving earth
and I find roses
blooming in the waist-high weeds

PASSING

hours
pass
days
pass
nights
pass

and yet the yearning for the light step
of the past
does not pass

when will the pain be erased?

the days
that heal
have not yet
passed

by me

I LOOKED IN THE MIRROR

I looked in the mirror
and I saw
 a damaged woman
damaged, like a broken-winged bird
that can no longer fly
damaged, like a fruit too spoilt to be eaten
damaged, like a woman too afraid to love

and I told myself
you can never get over it
you will never get over it
you should never get over it
like a mantra of disbelief in self,
these words haunted me

until the day when
my breath no longer tightened
in rounds of barbed wire across my chest
my voice no longer caught in my throat
my eyes no longer saw only scars in my reflection

and I was able to hear the words of wisdom
from deep within
that said
you don't need to get over it
this experience is part of you now
it is your beauty and your ugliness
your smiles and your sorrow

it marks the lifelines that others trace with trust
it lives within you and joins you
to every other soul who suffers

there is nothing;

there is
no
thing
to get over

and I looked in the mirror and saw

my   self

OH MY DARLING

oh my darling
I adore you

every wrinkle,
every line

how this ageing skin becomes you
life and love, sewn so fine

your skin's a tapestry of
what you've been through

stretch marks, scars and dimpled thighs
all the wealth of years is showing
in the fading of your eyes

if that blue is not so
bright now

if that strength in flesh and bones
eludes you, leaves you
leaves you wanting
I accept it - queen of crones

for the body as it falters
is no more or less than you
you in beauty, you in truth
you, in flaming, burning youth

now at last when bloom is fading
joints are aching, muscles slack
now I see you truly, deeply
now I see you nothing lack

now I see you

in the mirror

now when 60 years have passed
now I find what I was seeking
now I love you
first and last

Linnet with her autoharp, Maeve.

Linnet Hunter is a performance poet and creator of the Writers' Retreat Garden. From this space of shady trees, velvety petals and spicy scented herbs, nestled in a tiny town in the southwest of Victoria, Australia, she shares her love of words and her connection to the earth.

www.ingramcontent.com/pod-product-compliance
Lightning Source LLC
Chambersburg PA
CBHW022023290426
44109CB00015B/1288